# Between the Grey

## Poetry and Prose

JAMES COMPTON

**WRITERS REPUBLIC L.L.C.**
515 Summit Ave. Unit R1
Union City, NJ 07087, USA

**Website:** *www.writersrepublic.com*
**Hotline:** *1-877-656-6838*
**Email:** *info@writersrepublic.com*

Ordering Information:
Quantity sales. Special discounts are available on quantity purchases by corporations, associations, and others. For details, contact the publisher at the address above.


Library of Congress Control Number:     2020940871
ISBN-13:          978-1-64620-441-0      [Paperback Edition]
                  978-1-64620-442-7      [Digital Edition]


Rev. date: 07/06/2020

Cover Illustration by Francesca Steele

Thank you to my wonderful parents Caroline and Blake who have always taught me to believe in myself and push to be the best version of myself. I would also like to thank my little brother Mason who inspires me to better myself and let others hear our voices. Additionally thank you to all my grandparents who have encouraged me to share what I believe in. Finally thank you to my friends and everyone who had read my material and pushed me to do more with it, to name a few, thank you, Jacob, Michel, Micheal, Frankie, and everyone else who has taken this path with me.

Now as you read this, I believe you picked it up because you were meant to. It may be because you are looking for new ways to interpret life, or you may be hoping some words layed out elegantly will bring clarity to some of your confusion. Maybe you just like poetry, not realizing you love it because it takes you away into another version of you. No matter the reason, I ask one thing of you... try to find a way each piece of writing reflects a part of you and also a reason it may not. As I wrote these I discovered I loved doing this as it demonstrated that even I had reasons to disagree or embrace my own words when reading over them once more, even if the change was slight. Look for every view in these, and attempt to see how life is meant to feel as abstract, as unique to an individual as even the strangest poem.

Today every place
we look we see a
world that gets lost
within their own negativity,
stuck in either the future
or the past, but rarely
in the present.
If the people of the world
were to live as if today was
the only thing promised,
that the sun would not rise,
I believe everything would be
said.
Every feeling of love would be
spoken.
and every apology would be
forgiven.
True honesty would be achieved
for the first time since
a lie was discovered.
The world needs to begin
to enlighten each other
instead of hiding their individual
intricacies, everyone has
something to say
that nobody else has heard.

He asked us again,
Did the sun rise,
Yes, it did, it always does,
But still he always asked.

The question was always so sincere,
And the reaction is always a smile,
His only smile each day.
We didn't know.

Two more weeks went since he arrived,
Fourteen more mornings he asked,
She was rude today,
She said no.

He sat up, trying to stand,
But fell as he was too weak.
He then cried,
A wrinkled face pleaded to go outside.

Here, of course, he saw the sun rose,
Just as it always does,
He began to cry harder,
She finally asked why?

The response was gentle, but shaky
"My dear wife,
Told me this,"
He opened his mouth,
but paused.

"I will be gone soon,
But with each sunrise,
You will awake to me,
Looking into your eyes."

"Warming the world,
Just as you
Had once warmed by sad heart,
When I felt so cold."

And then we knew
The sun did not matter,
He was making sure he could tell her
good morning, and show her his smile.

Live today For
Even Yesterday
Was not promised

Live tomorrow For
Even Today
May End Suddenly

Live For You
As others words May be broken

Live
For memories For
Everyone who
Dreams of having yours

Live For
Tranquility And
Chaos

Most things broken,
Can be mended
With the right person
To heal a wounded heart.

He sat alone,
Under the shadow of a broken clock
Looking on in disbelief
That time was seemingly gone.
As no seconds passed,
He knew at last,
He should have looked without his eyes,
For without time,
The only thing that mattered
Was stagnant in his mind.

The trees stood,
Whispering to the moon,
The branches freezing,
The leaves a lowly brown,
But did the tree sit and wonder,
Reminiscing on last June?
Although life slowly faded,
Barren to mostly bark,
Each tree was still a sight to behold,
As even a tree,
Lacking leaves,
Is still strong,
Still standing bold.

Reach,
For something beyond tomorrow,
And exceeding the next year,
Reach,
Past the moon,
And then reach past every star,
Reach,
Farther than every boundary,
Past each fear,
Reach,
Not for them,
But for you
And only you.

If tomorrow doesn't come,
Are there words,
You still wanted to say?
Or has your truth
Been spoken
Your thoughts completely spread...
Or will they
Only exist
In the mind
Of someone dead?

Say them loud,
And always clear,
As for me...
Even one word
Left unsaid
Is my biggest fear.

"Why"

Why love her?

Because she's mine.. Or she was.

"Does she even know who you are?"

Yes.

"She can name your favorites?"

Favorites?

"Movies, song, book?"

No.

"Then I don't think she listened."

Or I didn't tell.

I told you I was scared,

You should know this little voice.

"I wish I didn't"

YOU were the one who told me not to,

That it would end up making me hurt.

"I was wrong, lost."

You made me miserable, in pain.

"Forgive me."

Yes, and I'll find us both strength.

The girl sat there, wide eyed,
Believing her lover had died.
He once had saved her.
But now he changed,
Almost deranged.
Not truly gone,
But she needed to move on.
Life is too short,
To sit and wonder,
If this man could avoid plunder.

Create your freedom,
break yourself,
find help beyond a broken mind.
Deserve love,
search out pain.
Look alive,
look beyond what you first see.

I reach my unwilling hand to your face,
Why didn't you turn?
WE knew the touch would hurt,
Knew your skin would burn.
Instead you let me caress your cheek,
And look upon your grey eyes,
Not my place,
To build you up,
Each time I touched,
It began to burn you down.
Here we are,
Once more,
Pretending to pull you into salvation.
Brush me away,
Stop wanting to stay,
Bite this hand that feeds you,
It does not feed food,
It only gives lies,
And here love cannot survive.

I had it all,
Lost in my own words.
The world fell.
Content with standing still,
I lost what made me,
Made me who I was.
I couldn't see it,
Each thought had become blinding.

The river,
Stood still,
No current,
No rapids.

The waterfall,
Did not drop,
No crash,
The world had paused.

Still,
Water stood,
No ripples,
No waves.

But then,
One raindrop fell,
And now,
Life moved on.

Smile,
Not to create happiness.
Smile,
Not to mask your pain,
Smile,
Just to remember how it feels.

For you have not smiled,
Since you lost your way.

Your smile is not with your teeth,
I mean for you to smile with your eyes.

They feel the world's bliss.
And the world fear, its pain.

A smile with the eyes,
Is the only thing truly sincere.

She was pretty,
And smart too,
Amazing beyond any word,
But he knew he was too weak,
No excuse to try,
It would be wrong,
He couldn't break someone,
Just because he wanted
A different type of song.

The child woke up,'
Sprinted down the hall,
Pitter
Patter
Echoed on the walls...
Breaking the morning silence,
She knocked on her mom's door.
Her mom scared,
Yelled who's there.
She whispered,,,
Mom,
I want pancakes.
The mind of a child,
Always so free.

When a tear falls...
Does it wonder why?

Or does it hang on to the cheek,
Not wanting to drop?

Although transparent, It drips in a fog.

**Not** knowing where its going,
Or why it is gone.

Why?
This question brings trouble, Or more,
It brings pain,
But it's the most important question, It keeps the world sane.
Why love? Why hate? Why go?
Why stay?
You'll never know, Unless you ask Why"

Broken,
Now fixed,
Life
Shows its hardest
Trick

And now you were suddenly gone,
off to sing your own song,
but I stayed and was
wishing you had too.
That you still sang our song,
but
that's not how this love turned to be.

I sat there on the phone, wishing that it
was okay to stay.

But my pain was hurting each memory
we had ever made.
Even washing you away.

I hate to believe this be the end,
But rather a form of growing,
Just as a friend.

My heart still belongs to you,
Even when I'm gone,
I can't imagine writing anyone else a
song.

I still picture us laying in bed,
Spreading out each dream,
Manifested in our head.
Maybe those dreams aren't really dead.

Now..

I have changed, I have grown.
It just took, being on my own.

I pray for you to finally see me,
This person i had a dream i could be

All I once did wrong, I can finally see,
and now
life can move along.

They say no expectations,
No sad sensations,
Life still goes on,
Nobody wants to admit this wrong
But in the eyes of empathy,
It is clear to see
How life is meant to be.

Would life be different,
If everyone lived only to love,
To grow together,
To find beauty,
Even if it was only found through risk.

I no longer crave a girls touch,
Or feel of her skin.
Not even to stare at her beauty.
I crave her mind,
To hear her soul come alive.

If one wish were to come true,
It would be to be blessed with you,
To lock onto your eyes,
And finally see,
What this world can truly be.

Last night,
I dreamed of you,
Standing in the sea,'
You smiled,
So mesmerizingly.
For life echoed with serenity.
In this dream though,
I was not there,
Yet when I awoke,
I loathed my eyes for opening,
And ridding my mind of you.
Something I had taken for granted,
When it was possible for you to stand before me.

Most nights
I have no choice
But
To try
And remember your sweet voice.
For I did not fall because of those
gorgeous eyes.
I did not fall for the way you smile.
I fell because each sound of your voice,
made me retreat from hell,
And find
A world of wonder.

I wish to dance inside your soul,
Where the light shines,
The times I feel restless.
I wish to walk inside your mind,
So I can see the thoughts of divinity.
I wish to be caught in the echo of your
voice just to feel a little bit of true
rejoice.
I wish to hold your pain in my palm,
and give it all to me,
Trap it away from you,
So your soul,
Your mind,
Your voice stay happy.

If the sun was dying
Would your last reach be to me?
Or would you simply die,
Without trying to be held closely?

I feel like i never lost her,
Simply because,
This version of me has never found her,
And she has never seen me.
We both saw a blueprint of what was
meant to be,
Not what life has now changed us to
see.

Truth is,
I used to always be broken,
Before and with you,
But the other truth is, without you,
I would have never grown strong.
Nine times out of ten,
We could heal each other for a brief
moment,
But oddly enough,
Ten made it permanent,
For ten made me see,
The person i needed to change to be,
To be the best version of me.
This one won't need healed at every
whisper of pain,
It finally knows what life should be,
My mind is healthy.
And I am strong.

Not all of you is trustworthy,
The mind can play a trick,
Your body can fake its own pain.
But the heart can be trusted,
As it yearns for all things good,
It cries to feel love, and happiness,
yet shatters when it feels broken.
So trust your heart when you feel lost,
It will guide you to tranquility.

We wish it was a simpler time,
These days we now live.
Everyone second guesses everyone
Especially how one feels.
If life was shorter, or even if we knew
when our time was up,
You would drive to her, or she would
call your number, maybe from memory.
Someone would pour their heart out,
free every thought driven from the
deepest part of their soul.
Tell everything they realize they did
wrong, but stand with what they did
right. Show they regret so much, but
also may change so little.
Not change the past because it led to
this moment.
A moment filled with transparency.

But

We live in this age, a dark age,
Where a simple feeling, and especially
the feelings most complex,
Are never heard by anyone,
Anyone, except our own tortured
minds.

This moment I declare peace.
I won't need another revelation for an
eternity, even I remain disclosed to.
I'll just need this,
This person I have created,
Will be delicate,
Yet strong.
They will understand there is a moment
for both.
And when the moment comes, they
intertwine,
it will be when I am complete.

Draining myself seemed to become a
passion that I could not stop.
Overthinking,
drowned me,
even though as I drowned deeper,
and deeper
into a dark abyss denser than water,
I just yelled how much I liked to swim.
Delusion.
Now I only think once,
trust my heart,
and my mind
to find a salvation of peace,
even if this brings a wrong answer.
It will stop what was once pain,
choosing to keep swimming with no air.

*No*

**Yes**

*I can't* **You can** *No*

**Yes**

*How*

**You are you. And**

**You are powerful.**

Everyone has this person that pops up
like a flower in the middle of a desert
and shows a new beauty to a life that
had been seen as barren. Yet they
become content with the view and
forget it was once the most vibrant part
of a shallow life.

If he were to come up to you and ask
you a question, what would you want it
to be?
Would you want him to ask about a
color that changed your life?
Ask if god saved you?
Question your purity to the world?
Maybe that should be one of the most
important things to look for, someone
who asks questions that allows you to
show the true version of yourself. A
question, you have to think about
before answering.

The day she said goodbye to his broken
soul was the day her soul began to
awaken. Rising out of a shadow to see a
shade of moonlight it had only dreamt
of seeing before.

I once washed my face,
With a hose outside within my garden,
because even the sight of a clean sink
reminded me of you when I needed to
think of myself.

Is a serene night worth a future of
heartache?
**20** nights of pure euphoria mixed with
your delightful grin,
Sadly could end,
Then **20** weeks of a melancholic flow
while you try to forget and learn how to
forgive.

You may only say one thing to truly
earn someone back in your life,
whether a partner or sibling, or parent.

You promise them, you will be real, and
nothing more.

Distant hearts
Do not
Deserve feeling
Despair

Fly me into the sky,
Where I will find a sunset,
And can breathe within a cloud,
I'll touch each fading ray of sun as they
drop into darkness.
Make me feel like a child again,
Ready to discover a world that
resembles beauty, at every glance.

Make it so I can be free,
Free from a past,
Where you And I,
Made this thing last,
Despite us always having to wear
A blank mask.

The rose
Bloomed
As the dew fell,
From an overlooking tree,
This rose,
The only one of its kind,
Did not belong in the woods,
Still,
It had found light,
Its place did not matter,
It was here,
Its purpose to bring beauty,
So why would it hesitate to bloom?

Send me the strength,
To always ask every question,
To ask for guidance,
When life leaves me lost.

Free the mind,
Even when you are angry,
And especially when you find a moment
to be content.
Show yourself a feeling you deserve.

If I went back and could leave myself a
note, it would be simple.

Never fail due to ignorance,
Never lose because you didn't find the
courage to ask.
Always find 3 reasons to smile.
Enlighten your mind,
Daily.
And finally,
Share what you have been taught.

One day,
These words won't mean a thing,
Even to me,
As I will also be gone too.

The saddest thought
I ever manifested,
Makes me sad because it's true.
How many words have we lost,
That brought power through elegance,
But didn't survive time?
Lost in a history, that doesn't always
favor salvation through knowledge.

When you grow old
You will have no regrets,
Even though you will be wrong an
infinite amount of times.
Because it's okay to be wrong, as long
as you tried to stay good, even when
you were wronged.

A whisper does not represent silence,
as even it has to break the peaceful air.
So why do people think they're too
small to shatter a world stuck in its
ways.
Stand for something,
as long as you keep believing in you.

Age doesn't dictate life,
Life goes on the very same,
A minute is a minute to everyone,
A second goes by forever,
So what does dictate life,
The answer so simple,
Manage every minute with care,
Make each minute a moment with
meaning.
A moment you would hate to missed.

Every night
When the sky starts to sparkle
through each star,
and the moonlight grows brighter,
I look up,
Trying to think of something other than
you.
But I never can,
And that's why I smile,
As the one part of this life,
I know we will forever share,
Is the beauty of the night sky.

Once in your life,
You don't want to be the one,
The one desperately confessing,
Confessing love that isn't deserved,
Or confessing you were wrong, when
deep down you know you aren't.
I know you,
You just want love,
But don't always realize what it may
cost.

Just try.

Please.

Try.

You do not have to succeed.

Try.

And if you need more than

encouragement.

Remember.

I love you.

It doesn't feel like it is true,
But one day you will be crowned,
As royalty,
As queen or king of your own life.
But does wearing this crown matter if
the one beside you, feels cast away.
Summoned to watch you rule from a
distance.
From a place where they do not stand
with you.
Rule you may,
Yet solitude met with desire,
Makes the feeling of royalty obsolete.
Those who admire, support, and cheer,
should not be away in any sense,
As you ascend to a darkened abyss,
Where you let your strength of
compassion,
Cease to exist.

Life is cracking
Beneath her feet
Memories breaking
Not breached
But there is a time
She will see
Every answer she needs.

The answer right there,
As it was always her.

To stand on her feet
To fight the world
Bring it to her knees
She has power
She can't seem to hold
But when she realizes
She is strong
She will bless everyone
Starting with herself

The sky falls dark,
An earlier time for you as you are far
away from home,
But that doesn't mean we don't share
the same sky.
You get light sooner this is true, but still
it fades long before mine.
Therefore we may never experience the
same light at the same time.

The rain started falling again,
Sliding across the falling leaves,
Onto the pavement,
Where it would lay until it dried.
The drops brought a picture,
A vision manifesting clarity,
To even the darkest landscape,
As they reflected what matters most.
You.

The teddy bear was a gift, from a father
she felt she had never truly met.
She still holds it so closely every night,
Dreaming of a man she used to see,
Hoping to see him again,
But he was gone.
Wishing to, it was possible to see her.

Don't fight for a lifeline,
Your life isn't here to be reliant on
someone else,
someone else to create your peace
and happiness.
Find your own serenity beyond the
shadows.
Your own reasons to smile.
For when you find a reason to laugh on
your own,
you will see you never needed a lifeline,
you just need yourself,
others come to enhance something
already great,
not to help you find good.

Goodnight to those who lay beside
someone else before, someday you will
move past and break free of your own
self placed curse,
but it won't be tonight.
Lay in the silence broken by the
memory of their voice,
Search for a sign that it wasn't your
fault,
or maybe for a sign it was.
Apologize to the ghost created by their
lingering fragrance within your sheets,
and give forgiveness if this scent
apologizes back.
Fill yourself with painful memories and
guide yourself finally to sleep.
When tomorrow comes you will wallow
more,
your mind will realign,
count your blessings in the morning
and forget the rest,
it's time for you to rise,
leaving the ashes of the past.

OKAYOKAYOKAY.... *Okayokayokay*
Brain.. She asked how we were today,
*I know... but I don't...*
Please figure it out, I can't do this here
*Fine... say you're fine, yes finefinefine*
Stop repeating, my heart is worrying.
*SorrySorrySORRY,*
*SHE HATES YOU NOW*
What? I haven't even answered.
*So?*
*weWEwe did something wrong.*
Brain turn off, im feeling strange
*If i turn off who will WORRYworry*
Nobody, please let me respond.
*NOnoNo, I control this.*
*Let her move on*
How can I break free of this?
*You can't.*

The words she said were not pretty,
in fact they stung when I recited them
inside my head.
But somehow when her voice let them
out, they sounded beautiful, as if she
was speaking a painting into existence.
Yet when I speak them now, not a single
word was close to a positive sound. No
euphoric feeling should have been felt.
They were so cruel,
Menacing, each syllable now burnt as it
rolled off a different tongue.
How could I be naive hearing this
before?
Making it seem like her voice was
captivating me to dance to an old song.
Blinding, that's what she has become.
After realizing this I stood in disbelief,
Trying to convince myself that she was
not capable of creating such
melancholic phrases designed to cut my
soul.
Now, I walk with care, and listen with
caution,
For if her voice was meaning with no
words, life wouldn't feel like being
trapped in a world of undertone.

As I lay here solitary
My mind does not feel alone
Each thought
Every memory
All of my dreams
Come to life as the night whispers
through its darkness.
It echoes for tranquility
And a bravado
To awaken inside of my head,
Creating a newfound strength to say
what i already should have said.
For I do not cry in angst,
Or yell in the feelings of despair.
Instead my emotions remember to be
cloying, to fill the air with idyllic auras.

Only now do I remember I am alone,
But tomorrow will be a mission,
To revel in the world, and see the
hidden kindness it has always had to
offer.

When my mind connected with its
spirit, I believe I have finally set myself
free.

Say goodnight,
To those you truly love

Say good morning to those you truly
miss

Say your truth to all,
For only those who deserve your
presence will respect your honesty.

I could tell that once you smiled,
But even now when you bare your teeth
Nothing else shines.
Yes,
It breaks my heart,
Even as you are just a **stranger**
I saw boarding the train and
Now I can't say that I'll bring a happy
version of you back,
I can't even say that I'll see you again,
But with your dark hazel eyes,
Maybe,
Oh just maybe
You'll read this and know that you're
worth it.
You would be worth bringing out of a
darkness I'll never know about.
Sincerely,
The **stranger.**

We all wish to be **heard**
But to be **heard**
We must understand what it means to
**listen**
Listen not just at every syllable but
listen beyond any sound,
To listen to the silence between each
sentence.
Between each breathe.

I had a revelation yesterday that I didn't
belong in this scene.
I did not like escaping alone from a
picture that was so solemnly desperate
to be someone nobody should strive to
be.
I've never truly met any of my friends,
I've just seen how well they can
pretend.

If you were to get a 10 second preview
of another person before you include
them in your life, would you watch it?
And if this went the same way for
someone before meeting you, would
they like what they saw?

You once left me a note saying you love me, but I don't remember my first time reading it, still it's stapled to my notebook, because it's from you.

Once a month we should all take 10
dollars and send it all away.
Four dollars to her,
Four dollars to him,
And two dollars to a stranger.
All with a note saying they're worth far
more than this.
Maybe that will empower them to be
even more.

Why do we get scared of the dark?
We never see a monster,
We are rarely out of someone's hearing.
We get frightened because only in dark
Do we fully listen to our own thoughts
Then pray the next night won't be as
full of turmoil between ourselves.

People want to be better?
Show me how?
No,
Don't point at what they're doing,
Show me yourself and
I'll show you through me.

If tomorrow failed to be better
and you knew this would be it's fortune,
would you still rise and fight?

Every time we breathe it's a miracle we
take for granted,
And still I chose to waste 300 breaths
forcing out tears for someone I once
missed.
300 breaths wasted,
300 miracles
spent focusing on a negative past.

Do we ever get over our first kiss when
everyone wears it as a crown?
No.
I propose we ask about their last,
to show something more recent to
make them see current love.

Breakfast
Cooked for you,
But you wouldn't get out of bed
I know it's Sunday and you are tired
But I tried so hard just for you,
So maybe next week you'll rise before it
gets cold,
And if not then maybe
My warmth for you will also start fading

Acknowledge the little things,
Like a stranger saying hello
You don't know if that was hard
Or a challenge they overcame
Say it back and smile,
The difference it can make,
May prevent an early escape.

Some people need to stop living in one
color,
There's nothing wrong believing the
grass is greener on the other side,
Many times it is,
But maybe green isn't what should be
looked for,
Greatness can be found in even grey.

I shrug, and tell myself good enough,
way to often,
And although I feel myself breaking,
From a self imposed let down,
It can get so hard to stop this habit.

Honesty over everything,
Even over humility,
If you're the best and don't own it,
You're letting someone else believe
they're beating you,
Be honest and build confidence,
Confidence maintains strength,
And strength will breed a better you.

Free us, free us, oh cracked hands,
Let go of our strings,
And let us have our own plans,
You think us no good,
So you restrain our breath,
Free us, free us, oh cracked hands.
One day I'll break away from your
horrid grasp, to a freedom,
Unhindered by the past.

Driving alone, with the music low,
I finally grew strength to let you go,
Until I heard a song you once sung,
Each word echoing off the glass,
As if you still sang next to me,
I tried to turn it down, but could not
turn the dial,
I knew deep down i had to listen,
But to sing in my own tune,
Off key I cried out,
Messing up each word,
I fought, strangling my mind,
To decide if this was the fate,
We deserved.

How could anyone believe in another
person, when all we do is seem to lose
them?
We try to bring out good, maybe for the
wrong reasons, but still
Goodness is needed to fight away pain.
Still we throw so much away.

If I caught a stranger struggling for life
I would do anything to help.
Get over my fear of blood, to stop them
from bleeding.
Give them my air,
To ensure they're breathing,
And almost anyone would do the same,
But what we fail to realize is the
stranger who may be dying, but could
live without us struggling to help,
All it takes is a few positive words,
Or even a smile as you open a door,
Those fighting their mind,
Deserve a hidden remedy,
To help fight their hidden scars.

When I see a deep black, I don't see
darkness anymore,
I see the mystery of all the colors in
one, and wonder if each one of them is
trying to break free.
Blue reaching to once again unite with
the sky above,
Green struggling to bring its brightness
to the tree.
Red climbing back to the sunset it left
behind.

Shielded from the fires,
The monster sat staring at the party,
Chanting for it's life,
It had never tried to bring pain,
To make there be fear.
The monster had just tried to live,
But became outcasted to the night.

Rain is the most peaceful sound,
The splash as it hits the ground,
So genuine,
Almost sweet,
But still the raindrop had to break to
make us hear that sound,
So we may have to break,
For our voices to be heard.

I once saw a girl that made me rethink
life itself,
She was so beautiful,
And truth is I didn't need to see her
eyes
Or the way her nose scrunched to see it
I could see it in the way she moved,
Clumsily but with grace,
Contradicting anything I'd seen before,
She didn't try to move a certain way,
Or care that I was looking her way.
She just moved,
Free
Free from anything the world had once
declared she must strive to be.

Stripes confuse me,
I see them as lines wanting to evolve
but switching back to something of
their past,
Maybe they confuse me because they're
So consistently inconsistent.
Or maybe
I
Have
No
Sense
Of
Style

Writing essays was always easy,
All I had to do was write like others
talk,
Make a lie sound truthful,
Make it sound like im an expert on
someone or something I have never
dreamed of understanding.
Poetry is different, it has to come from
within, and it is always unique, and true
because words reflecting meaning are
always sincere.

I want to break again,
Last time I did I felt reborn,
Maybe this next time I break,
I will be able to be fearless.

You don't have to have a burning desire
to show her love,
But if any part of you chooses to love
her, do it with everything you have,
Believe me,
The worst pain comes from knowing
you could have loved her harder.

You left your hairbrush by my bed,
And I want to call you to give it back,
But that means hearing your voice,
Looking at the brush and reliving the
memory of you beside me is one thing,
but hearing your voice,
The sweet voice I still love,
Will drive me back to yesterday.
The day before I had to leave,
The day we stopped being you and me.

As the new century arises,
And last year's night falls,
I fell in love,
Not with a beautiful girl,
But with the future me,
Someone who grew,
And learned what it means to be.

The snow fell for the first time in years,
I had forgotten what this was,
For a moment in time,
My world grew so silent,
And I could actually hear my voice,
I heard it say I matter,
Something rarely heard before,
It just took the snow,
To capture all the exterior noise,
And oddly nothing more.

One day I'll crawl out of bed and feel
like taking over the world, I'll go out
and find myself the most wonderful
girl, and she'll sing to me and tell me
how I'm wonderful,
But that is not today,
My room is still cold,
My light is so far away,
But I keep telling myself,
Tomorrow will be the day.

A robin landed next to me as I sat on a
chair, I felt so alone until it gracefully
landed there, I sat almost still but with
a wandering gaze, the robin had eyes
that could fill a soul with love, she sat
there even more as if she had no reason
to fly, and I sat there too, wondering if
this girl would listen beyond me saying
hi.

Don't underestimate
The power of standing alone,
How can you feel weak,
When no one can tell you you're wrong
Speak kindly to yourself,
And also aloud,
For you must be the greatest,
In a one person crowd.

What would my life be if I slept in that
one morning,
And hadn't seen the sunrise.
Would I still understand beauty,
Or my love for the arts?

I hate my love for blue eyes,
They captivate me,
And I really can't explain why,
They don't remind me of a chocolate
daze as deep brown do,
They don't show me the melodies hazel
describes.
Maybe I love them for one simple
reason,
They appear nearly clear,
Like i can see into this person.

I have a scar under my eye from when I
was four,
I fell off my deck,
That"s all I remember,
But I believe to this day,
That my eye was not hurt,
And the scratch wasn't an inch higher,
Just so both my eyes could see you
In this moment.

Crying is the most pure of any act,
It can show the saddest moment,
Yet the most happy,
Never ignore someone crying in front
of you,
Whether they are full of despair,
Or joy,
They found the strength to let you see
their tears.

Last birthday
I wished to find peace
I knew I could eventually see it in
myself
But I didn't need to wait,
I found it within you.

I'm not the strongest,
Nor the most intelligent,
I may not be the best at anything,
Yet I thank the universe, as it let me
see,
I have purpose beyond a gift,
I am here to make happiness exist.

Nothing
Hurts
More
Than
Choosing
Ignorance

As we drove through the storm,
I was not scared,
Your hand lay inches from mine,
And that,
Was all I needed

Here you are, you made it to the end, be
proud of that, anytime you finish
something be proud. It shows your
persistence, and grows the strength you
have within.
There are now just a few words left to
read, and please, take them with you
when you close the cover.

Make yourself a happy moment
everyday

Try to express your identity in a way
that even you haven't seen before

Cry,
I mean it, not because of sadness.
Find the best memory you wish to
relive, picture it so vividly that a tear
runs down your chin. My memory is
with a lost grandparent.

Don't surrender to feeling hopeless,
there is always hope somewhere, and if
you can't find it in the world, find it
within me.

Smile, even if it feels forced today, it
will feel more natural tomorrow.
Eventually it will be hard not to smile.

Keep loving and never stop.

This world loves you even in your
darkest days. Embrace what makes you
who you are.

CPSIA information can be obtained
at www.ICGtesting.com
Printed in the USA
LVHW040806021120
670425LV00007B/405